Creating Dynamic Organizations

FT Prentice Hall
FINANCIAL TIMES

In an increasingly competitive world, we believe it's quality of thinking that will give you the edge – an idea that opens new doors, a technique that solves a problem, or an insight that simply makes sense of it all. The more you know, the smarter and faster you can go.

That's why we work with the best minds in business and finance to bring cutting-edge thinking and best learning practice to a global market.

Under a range of leading imprints, including *Financial Times Prentice Hall*, we create world-class print publications and electronic products bringing our readers knowledge, skills and understanding which can be applied whether studying or at work.

To find out more about our business publications, or tell us about the books you'd like to find, you can visit us at www.business-minds.com

For other Pearson Education publications, visit www.pearsoned-ema.com

PEARSON
Education

Executive Briefings

www.briefingzone.com

Creating Dynamic Organizations

Human capital issues and options for tomorrow's business

MIKE JOHNSON

FT Prentice Hall
FINANCIAL TIMES

An imprint of Pearson Education

London • New York • Toronto • Sydney • Tokyo • Singapore
Hong Kong • Cape Town • Madrid • Paris • Amsterdam • Munich • Milan

PEARSON EDUCATION LIMITED

Head Office:
Edinburgh Gate
Harlow CM20 2JE
Tel: +44 (0)1279 623623
Fax: +44 (0)1279 431059

London Office:
128 Long Acre
London WC2E 9AN
Tel: +44 (0)20 7447 2000
Fax: +44 (0)20 7447 2170
Website: www.briefingzone.com

First published in Great Britain in 2003

ISBN 0 273 66358 5

British Library Cataloguing in Publication Data
A CIP catalogue record for this book can be obtained from the British Library.

10 9 8 7 6 5 4 3 2 1

Typeset by Monolith – www.monolith.uk.com
Printed and bound in Great Britain by Ashford Colour Press Ltd, Gosport, Hants.

The Publishers' policy is to use paper manufactured from sustainable forests.

About the author

Mike Johnson is a consultant and author and managing partner of Johnson & Associates, a corporate communications consultancy he founded in 1982. In addition to his consulting activities he is the author of *Talent Magnet: Getting talented people to work for you* (2002) and *Winning the People Wars* (2000) both published by Financial Times Prentice Hall; *Managing in the* NEXT *Millennium* (1995) (translated into 11 languages); and *Getting a* GRIP *on Tomorrow* (voted one of the 30 best business books in 1996). Two other books on teleworking and outsourcing were published in co-operation with the Institute of Management in 1997. In 1998 he created and developed the highly acclaimed global study *Building and Retaining Global Talent: Towards 2002* for the Economist Intelligence Unit. He is a frequent speaker and chairman at business functions, conferences and seminars on human resources and organizational strategy issues and has worked extensively with both large multinationals and international consulting groups and institutions.

Mike can be contacted at the following address:

Mike Johnson
Little Buckland Farm
Hollywood Lane
Lymington
Hampshire
SO41 9HD

Tel: 01590 688899
E-mail: mikeajohnson@compuserve.com

Contents

Executive briefing

THE RESEARCH PROCESS

The purpose of the report is to investigate present and future human resource issues in corporations in Europe and the United States, specifically related to the recruitment, reward and retention of talented teams and individuals.

The research process was based on four basic approaches:

- Individual, face-to-face interviews in Europe and the United States.
- Group discussions in Europe and the United States.
- Telephone and e-mail interviews.
- Desk research on developing human resource issues.

More than 70 senior managers from major corporations were interviewed face-to-face. They included chief executives, general managers, human resource managers, strategic planning experts and business consultants specializing in human resource issues.

The interview process took place from October 2002 to February 2003, with the main interviews being conducted in person by the author in Atlanta, New York, Philadelphia, Amsterdam, Brussels, Frankfurt, Geneva, London, Paris and Zurich.

From the outset of the research, a policy of *off-the-record* interviews was established and strictly maintained throughout. On that basis we accorded every interviewee *complete anonymity* and consequent total confidentiality. Our reason for doing this was that we wanted our discussion to reflect the real human resource issues in the corporations of Europe and North America, not the company line in the annual report or web site. Indeed, our participants were asked for their personal views based on their career experiences and not necessarily their current position. The only reference to the corporations is a listing of the companies from whom we drew our interviewees.

We are confident that the seniority and experience of our select group of participants presents an accurate reflection of human resources issues and provides true insight into the options and opportunities for human resources management in the future.

Preface

There comes a point in every investigative project of this kind when you finally 'break the code' and realize just what all the interviews and desk research are really telling you. To be honest, after four months of face-to-face discussions, round-table-sessions and telephone interviews, there was a distinct tendency to be depressed. Depressed by the state of private enterprise on both sides of the Atlantic; depressed about much of the cynicism I had encountered; depressed about whether the collective power of corporate Europe and America was really bothering investing much in an eventual recovery as far as human resources were concerned.

I discussed my pessimism and the pessimism of the market with several colleagues and they urged me to have another look at the evidence I had assembled. I am relieved I did. While there is much to deride corporations for in their inability to cope with downturns, there are some (perhaps more than we think at first glance) who are making plans for the future; plans that do involve their people.

What I decided, as I began to write this book was that it needed to have a positive ending and that is what I have done. While I have made no attempt to hide the hole private enterprise dug for itself over these past two years, I felt that the most value I could bring, was to highlight those who are getting it right. More than that, to give useful examples and advice for anyone concerned with readying their business for tomorrow.

This book is about human resources and the role human capital will play in the creation of the next generation of dynamic organizations. It is my belief that without our human capital in great shape we will lack the wherewithal to succeed in the quest for a better business model. In the past months we have seriously downgraded our human resources and, consequently, our collective reputation as employers is not what it used to be. If we want – and we will – to once again attract and retain talent – both collectively and individually – we are going to have to play by a new set of rules. What I have tried to explain in this book are some of those new rules and how business needs to deal with them.

Most important of all, the human factor in our businesses will once again dominate. To succeed, we are required to look at the human issues of our organizations in a positive, proactive fashion. This book has one aim, to help you, the reader, do that.

Creating Dynamic Organizations: Human capital issues and options for tomorrow's business is about facing reality. It is something all of us in business

need to do right now if we are to build new businesses – that can confidently face the future – secure in the knowledge that their access to human capital will be undiminished for the simple reason that they are great places to work.

Acknowledgements

Individuals from the following organizations were interviewed for the book.

A.C. Neilsen

A.T. Kearney

Accenture

Alstom

ASML

Association of Executive Search Consultants

Avon

Base

Belgacom

Bristol Myers Squibb

British Telecom

Campbells Soup

CDI

Center for Creative Leadership

CIGNA

Cisco Systems

Citigroup

Conference Board

Coutts

DBM

Deloitte Touche

Delta Airlines

Dexia Bank

DHL

Dresdner Bank

Echo Communications Research

Economist Intelligence Unit

EDS

Egon Zehnder
Ernst & Young
Euroclear
ExxonMobil
Federal Express
Financial Executives International
Fortis
GE Capital
Godiva
Hewitt
Hoffman Associates
Honeywell
HR Gateway
Interbrew
Korn-Ferry
Lehman Brothers
Lenox
Manpower
MasterCard
Mercer
Middle East Management Centre
Nestlé
Novartis
Novell
Oxfam
Palm
Pepsi-Cola
Personal Journeys
Philips
PricewaterhouseCoopers
Proctor & Gamble
Richmond Events
Right Consultants

SN Brussels

Strategic Practices Group

SWIFT

Technitrol

The Life Coaching Company

Theron

Towers Perrin

Toyota

UBS

Zurich Financial Services

1

Looking to the organizational future

INTRODUCTION

With corporate America and corporate Europe still mired in recession, it is all too easy to reflect the depression being felt by many. This recession has been long and deep and has affected most of us at the same time, regardless of geography or industry. Worse still, it has been the 'unseen' recession. It has crept upon us without us really noticing. Major business events like the Dot.com meltdown and the corporate governance scandals, that rocked the establishment on both sides of the Atlantic, meant that as thousands were laid off it didn't make the usual headlines. Countries on a war footing and fighting global terrorism pushed all but the very biggest business stories to the back pages.

Of course we now know that 2001, 2002 and 2003 will go down as one of the worst economic recessions ever, and that it will be remembered for the terrible human toll it wrought as thousands upon thousands of workers found themselves in 'career transition', to use the euphemism of the outplacement industry.

So, is there any good news? That depends where you look. Some say that few have learned any lessons at all, and simply reverted to type: the 'hire and fire' mentality taking over once again. There is certainly plenty of evidence for that – even among the smart organizations. But it would be too easy just to dismiss this recessionary period as a time when no one learned anything at all. As our investigations have shown, many corporations have used this economic downtime to look *very* closely at where they go next. Even those that faced the trauma of first-ever downsizings (think telecommunications, think high-technology) have, in many cases, moved forward. And that, it would seem, is a good thing.

Because, in our interviews for this book, it became obvious that by early 2001 many of our businesses were:

- top heavy: there were just too many people to be sustainable in even the shortest downturn;
- in a talent-driven bubble (where even the talentless were being hugely rewarded) that needed serious correction;
- unaware of what uncontrolled greed can do;
- unable to see the signs of a slow-down and unwilling to believe it anyway: mass self-delusion was seriously in vogue.

Every executive in every corner of the globe has paid the price for those oversights in the intervening months and years. But what did the meltdown of our corporate economies really do? The answer to that depends on where you work, who you work for and what they, or you, have learned. It is also about something a lot

more fundamental. The search for talent never really went away. We are still short of those mythical 'good' people, who can change any business.

What this means is that come the upturn, we are going to be short of people once more. The thought then is, 'how many of my people are going to stay after their experiences with our firm in the recession?' and 'how many people will want to come and work here?'.

The problem is that sometime since 2001, many of us forgot that it would get better again. Our research shows that we are not going back to 'business as usual' come the upturn. We are going to have to accept that there are some new rules of business reality. All of them have a single common denominator – people. If we have got it wrong these past months, we are going to have a tough uphill fight to build some credibility: but we can do it. If we continue to get it wrong, there is no way your sales, your growth, your share price is going anywhere.

Over the past months, there's been a subtle shift in what employees expect and intend to get. All of us in business, whether we act as the employee or the employer, need to understand that. Without understanding and acting on these shifts and their consequent expectations we will not be able to recruit, reward and retain the people we need. That is the fundamental basis of this book.

From our interviews in North America and Europe, one message is glaringly obvious: there's a new way of working that will be the economic meeting ground of both smart employers and cynical employees. It has its roots in the boom times of the late 1990s, when a few implemented the concepts, but they were never widely adopted – despite glowing articles in the business press. They are built on a few cornerstones that will affect the way both employer and employee see the world of work:

- flexibility of employment
- focus on diversity
- new definitions of reward and recognition
- reinvention of trust in the workplace
- reputation and responsibility
- effective management of expectations
- new organizational structures.

There may be more than this. But these are the ones that kept being repeated in all our interviews. Some participants described them better than others, some were more enthusiastic, some were doubtful they would take hold in the short term, but all-in-all it isn't an overstatement to expect that these developments will

happen. Some corporations will lead and some will follow, but within a decade these seven – human resource related – issues will revolutionize our businesses.

This book will spend a lot of time on these, and related issues, their impact and how to organize your business for them. To give us some idea of how far ranging and how influential they will be let's take a quick, introductory look at each of them.

Before that, take one thing on board. These are not set in stone and they won't always be called what we call them here. Suffice to say that there is a revolution, it is real, it is energized by technology, the fall-out of globalization and the realization by an increasing majority of workers that there are other ways of doing the same thing – better. None of these issues stand alone, in fact they all, one way or another, impact and impinge on each other. For example the need for flexible employment requires a new look at rewards and how we manage people's expectations; maintaining trust involves corporate responsibility and the consequent reputation of our business. All of these issues interlink, all of them are current concerns for leading human resource practitioners and commentators who we talked to for this book.

Whether in Atlanta, New York, London, Brussels or Zurich, the leaders of tomorrow's business revolution (for that is what many of them are) are getting ready to play a new game of business, where employer and employee set and live by a new set of ground rules. Our view, borne out by our research, is that while many businesses are already tackling some of these as stand-alone issues, few are looking at all of these in any consistent or holistic fashion. But it is the recognition that *all* of these are critical issues coupled with the ability to put them all together and make them work, that will define who wins and who loses in the next corporate game.

Of course, the people boosters *will* say that these are *the* critical issues – they well might be. However, basic management principles within marketing, finance, logistics, production, R&D and so on will still be part of the equation. What, however, has come to the fore in our research on both sides of the Atlantic is that people are really going to make a difference this time. If you want to hire and hold the right people, you had better memorize this list and get to work on it.

FLEXIBILITY OF EMPLOYMENT

There's been a focus on flexibility of employment before (everything from telecommuting, job sharing, part time and sabbaticals). Our research shows that what has already happened is merely the tip of a huge iceberg. People everywhere

are redefining their lifestyle (that includes workstyle too) and will self-select employers on the basis of how they want to build their jobs and their careers. Employers who are not open to drastic changes in how people contribute to the business are going to starve themselves of the very talent they need to succeed. While these trends have already begun to embed themselves into certain locations (e.g. major centres of population), they are quietly manifesting themselves around the globe. Without our best efforts (aided by available, cheap technology) to understand and meet the needs of individual employees (needs that will change at different times in their careers), we will never be able to rely on long-term retention.

> *In the US today, I think that people are a lot less willing to move. I am shocked about how difficult it is to get people to move even in this present climate.*
>
> Strategic planner, Telecommunications industry.

And we are not just talking here about days off or extra vacation time. Longer lifespans and trends to have children later, for example, mean that many workers inherit both childcare and elder care simultaneously. Employers, therefore, have a choice: help employees tackle these difficult periods of their lives in a sensible way that still lets them make a useful contribution, or watch them make their own set of choices that don't include your business. Similarly, demographics in most of the US and Europe, mean that employment of the over-60s is not going to be a nice, 'social' thing to do, but a necessity.

Elsewhere – especially in our cities – single parents form a significant portion of the population. Finding sensible work patterns for these people can get much needed talent back into the workplace. Those that take the lead in these types of initiatives are going to be the winners of the twenty-first century.

FOCUS ON DIVERSITY

Most major corporations are a living, breathing mirror of their origins: that has to change. Minorities, whether from a sex, religious or ethnic orientation are going to be the lifeblood of our businesses in the future. But we need to manage that diversity far better than we do at present. Right now many Fortune 500 corporations are literally starving themselves of highly talented individuals by not embracing ethnic diversity – particularly in the senior executive ranks.

Our research shows that those who have an unambiguous attitude to diversity will win the race to recruit top talent. And pointing to the few that do, it doesn't really

help much. With just three women CEOs in the Fortune 500, corporate America is telling the story itself: it is no better on ethnic or religious grounds either. Don't think that we are picking on the US – Japan and the rest of Asia is far worse, and the French, Germans and Italians don't do well either. The only nations that have made progress are those in Scandinavia, the Netherlands and the UK, although there are signs that in all of these the trend is slowing down or reversing.

We stress again. In the future, we won't have a choice, get working at this now.

NEW DEFINITIONS OF REWARD AND RECOGNITION

In Europe and the US we have badly screwed up the reward system. We either paid too much or promised too much in, by now, worthless stock. Now we have halted all that and employees have worked out that toiling 70 hours a week today doesn't bring more money, more promotion or any guarantee of job security. This leaves us with an interesting question as business begins to take off again: 'will we be able to motivate by money?'.

> *We have depleted the reserves of the past and the optimism of the future.*
>
> General manager, FMCG industry

Our view is that this is one of those subtle changes that have already taken place. Indeed, balancing work and family is already the number one priority in the US and most European countries according to polls in 2002.[1] So the concept of reward is not going to be just about remuneration in the employer/employee work contract of the future. And – before they complain – it is the employers who have created this new set of rules for themselves, by a strictly boom and bust policy on pay and benefits. Pension and medical benefits have been slashed to ribbons in Europe and the US (it is estimated that up to a third of working Americans have no health insurance), with the new mantra that it is 'the employees' responsibility to save for the future'. Of course, there will always be those few for whom the idea of making a lot of money is *the* driver. There is no evidence that will ever entirely go away. But, for Mr and Ms Average employee – 70 per cent of whom (surveys tell us)[2] already think there is an unhealthy balance between work and

1. Finding time for family is a more pressing concern than being jobless. A Randstad survey in the US discovered that almost three times as many employees said family is their 'top priority' as those who listed work as a top priority.
2. *TrueCareers* (2002). US, Virginia: Reston. November.

personal life – reward is not going to be just about 'how much I take home each month and what my final pension will be'.

We said subtle shifts in the expectation of rewards by employees? Let's rephrase that. Let's make the suggestion that the reward package is going to be broader and deeper than ever before – and compensation experts who don't understand this are going to be very quickly out of a job. First, rewards and what they are will be a strategic decision taken by the CEO and his team and will set the style of the business, who works there and who tries to beat a path to your door. Yes, there will be some money in there, we all have to eat. But increasingly the package will be defined by the person you wish to hire and hold, their current status, their current needs and what you want them to achieve in the future.

Geographic location will be part of the reward strategy, because it will be a driver for those who want to work for you. Ease of transportation and housing (assisting with both counts too) are also a part. Office location (or lack of it), available equipment, flexitime and access to 'lifestyle' facilities (clubs, hotels, spas, vacation spots, free travel, airport lounges, weekend car hire) will also count. Is it happening now? Yes, it is. Is it very common? No. But technology allows us to treat and reward people in new ways and to change those packages as a person's needs change (the 1970s love affair with 'cafeteria compensation' comes close).

For example, if a 35-year-old executive, who is a key player in your future business plans, gets married (location needs and housing needs change) and has children (schooling needs, healthcare and vacation periods become a priority), his lifestyle doesn't subtly change it is subject to seismic shock. As his lifestyle undergoes a major upheaval his overall reward structure needs a total makeover.

All our discussions in Europe and the US point to the fact that if we are going to recruit and retain the right people, we will have to ratchet up the concept of reward to include a whole group of intangibles that become part of an evolving package. How do we do this? We are going to have to – depending on the business we are in and the business we want to be in in the future – decide just how many people get what part of the reward process. In some extreme cases (a top-end consultancy or a high-technology incubator firm) it might be everyone. In others, it might just be those high-potentials you must hold onto.

> *We bring in people who are integrators. We want people who will work in teams, not crazy stars.*
>
> CEO, marketing-led business.

Whatever your decision, it is going to take some revolutionary thinking to build this concept to reality, bearing in mind that by doing so you are also building a

platform for the culture of the firm (this is part of what it will be known for, it becomes part of the reason employees come to work). As business picks up, firms around the globe are going to move in this direction, it will be a way to effectively capture people by rewarding them with a lot more than monetary reward: underpinning who they are and who they aspire to be. Taking that further, leadership style, it could be argued, is also an intrinsic part of the reward package, because it is a major part of the workplace culture: the 'W' in work–life balance.

REINVENTION OF TRUST IN THE WORKPLACE

There's been a lot of talk recently about rebuilding trust between employer and employees. A great number of business commentators say that corporations have totally destroyed the trust equation by the way they treated (or mistreated) their employees over the past two or three years. Truth is that they are probably correct. Trust is at an all time low, for the very reason that few employees believe what they are told by their managers any more. This is on the basis that they don't think their managers know what is going on anyway; and they don't trust the CEO either.[3] The corruption and mismanagement scandals of 2002 were just the icing on the cake, putting business at its lowest level of popularity since the Industrial Revolution. Proof, if more were needed, lies in a December 2002 poll by broadcaster CNN, that found less than 17 per cent of Americans rated business executives highly (down from 25 per cent a year previous).[4] So has it broken the basic element of trust? Yes it has.

Two examples point to this:

1 Nearly twice as many employees in the US took sick days for personal need in 2002 as in 2001.

2. A Swiss banker – whose boss had just been given a $6 million golden handshake on the back of bringing the business to its knees – said that secretaries were beginning to steal office supplies to take them home for the children, 'And who can blame them?,' he said.

---

3 In a 2002 Watson Wyatt survey 'WorkUSA' only 39 per cent of workers said they trusted senior leaders at their firms.

4 CEOs and other executives can take comfort from the fact that they are not the worst: telemarketers at 6 per cent and car salesmen at 5 per cent fared worse.

If any further evidence was needed, a survey in late 2002[5] summed it up.

Have you witnessed a decline in employee trust over the past 5 years?

Yes	63.9 per cent
No	31.1 per cent
Not stated	5.0 per cent

Do you believe that employee trust is an issue for your firm?

Yes	77.3 per cent
No	19.3 per cent
Not stated	3.4 per cent

Over the next five years, do you predict employee trust will:

Decline	21.8 per cent
Stay the same	35.3 per cent
Increase	37.0 per cent
Not stated	5.9 per cent

But, while some say that employees will exact a bloody revenge for that lack of trust in the workplace come an economic upturn, there are others who believe that this isn't so. Even in corporations that have declared mass redundancies due to parlous times, there is a belief that if you did the whole thing right, then people can still be motivated and can still trust those at the top.

But many of us will need to act soon, as we are already losing people – not to competition but to other lifestyle options. There is strong evidence in both the US and Europe that talent is leaving for jobs in other sectors to just 'get away from business'.

Several managers we discussed the trust issue with said that the word 'trust' was wrong. 'It's not about trust, but about creating credibility', said one. 'Of course, we get it wrong sometimes and of course if the market is down we have to make decisions we don't like. But I believe that if you are seen to be fair in your dealings with those that have to go, you can still come out of it all OK.' Others pointed to

5 Survey of 250 HR managers attending the Richmond Events European Human Resources Conference in October 2002.

the fact that 'fostering a climate of real accountability' was a way to get everyone to trust each other.

Then again, talking to a senior manager in the high-technology sector his view was that 'creating your business based on the ability of teams, that are rapidly assembled and given urgent tasks to do, quickly develops trust across an organization'. He added, 'The trust process becomes natural, people either trust each other or not and you quickly sort out those you cannot really deal with, that means the business as a whole self-selects who stays and who goes. Once that has been achieved you are left with a group that trust each other and by that factor alone trust the firm.'

In another example, a US consulting firm says that it lives by the phrase, 'Demonstrate, don't Declare'. That, it says, underscores exactly what it is all about and expects management to live that on a daily basis. 'Our view is that managers from the top down, have to show how it's done and it is seen to be done. We find that this gives us a very close relationship with our employees.'

Again in the high-technology sector the idea of having the internal communications strategy driven by the top three executives seems to work – for them at least. Employees recognize the intrinsic honesty of the communication's process (if internal communications is run by human resources often – especially in a crisis – no one believes what is being fed to them). Also a clear hands-on, no bullshit approach, that can see any of the top team dropping into a junior employees office for coffee. 'In our firm that's normal', says the VP of human resources, 'it is an excepted and admired part of how we do business.'

But there are dissenters who consider today's businesses still too scared and too hungry. 'I am not sure how loyal people are going to be when the upturn comes', says a former general manager in the telecommunications industry, 'they won't feel that they are part of anything or that their contribution really matters.' He adds, 'My view, is that what corporations want today is people with contacts. They are not looking for loyalty or trust, they want to know what you know, then you can leave!'

Equally though, there are those who don't think it is about trust or loyalty at all. As several managers we interviewed pointed out, maybe all this talk about trust is just naïve in today's business world. As an alternative, all cited Jack Welsh's GE model. 'What he said', explained one manager, 'was, I am not looking for loyalty, I *am* looking for the best ten years of your career. In turn I will give you everything to make you the very best.' He continued, 'of course other corporations tried it, but they never really made it work. Basically, I think they never realized that the part GE committed to, and followed up on, was the "we will prepare you" for when you move on.' He added, 'well maybe it was a type

of trust, but it certainly worked and still does. Everyone knew just where they were, it was a clear cut bargain'.

You know, some of us have finally realized that you can't put one over on the troops. Hey, they are just as smart as we are.

CEO, Telecommunications industry.

While some suggest you can buck the anti-trust trend and get your employees committed again, 'even after you have been throwing rocks at them for a couple of years', the smart money doesn't really think so. 'What we are looking at now', says a Vice President (VP) human resources in the fast moving consumer goods (FMCG) sector, 'is engaging the people in the work they do. We think if we can get them knowing they are making a contribution we cannot ask for much more right now.' Others support that view. 'Despite some severe downsizing we have worked very hard to ensure that employees still see us as the best, or one of the best places they can work.' They added, 'whether this is true or not we won't know until the upturn comes and they start getting offers from our competitors'. All recognize one sobering fact, the more you are seen as a great place to work, the more you will be targeted by your rivals, because they know the employability of the talent you have.

Despite all this hard work to turn the trust equation into a positive experience, most companies seem to feel that this is a tenuous issue at best. All that can be done is give those employees a reason to come to work and make that much needed contribution. A hard nosed view from a Brussels-based manager in the pharmaceuticals industry, 'We had better not need trust any more, because it doesn't exist. We as employers broke the code of trust by injudicious downsizing, so trust has no economical value anymore.'

Then of course trust, loyalty and credibility are all ephemeral and can be quickly destroyed. Consider recent acquisitions, where the incumbent CEO, has built a great culture and has attracted talent to the firm by his actions and reputation. When these people are let go and another type of corporate culture is introduced this also destroys trust. 'People go to a job for all sorts of reasons, but they quickly feel a climate change', says one senior manager. 'Where a culture of trust is destroyed, you can watch it implode slowly. It usually takes two or three years at the headquarters (usually because of retention bonuses to hold key managers), and three to five years in the subsidiaries. After that it's all gone. Sadly, that has been the reality in too many firms and for too many employees.'

Of course if you have spent part of the downturn thinking through your firm's strategy for the next business cycle, that process – as long as employees are

sharing in it – automatically sends the right signals that you are trying to build a firm where people and their future aspirations count.

Our view is that if you don't have trust it can be very expensive and time consuming to build it. Better to find ways to fully engage your people and to be as honest, open, clear and consistent in your communication as you can, rather than talk too much about trust. Another thing, if you don't communicate well you cannot expect employees to believe too much of what you say, especially if you contradict yourself or keep changing the message. At the end of the day it is all about how you treat people, do you value them or not? Believe us they know.

Five key points to remember in all this:

- Treat people as adults, that's what they are.
- Communicate as honestly and openly as you can.
- Listen to your employees, it's surprising what you'll hear.
- Share your vision of the future.
- Make them know they are contributing.

REPUTATION AND RESPONSIBILITY

In every interview and every round table for this report, the importance of reputation as a recruiting and retention tool was stressed. It would seem there is little doubt that a firm's reputation is a vital part of the overall armoury required for long-term survival. However, just as reputation has come to the very forefront it has also become ever harder to maintain. Today a reputation for being a 'great place to work' can become tarnished practically overnight. All it takes is some bad news in one corner of a business empire and it quickly taints the whole corporate machine. The reality is that if you want to maintain a reputation that will attract and retain the people you need, you are going to have to spend a lot more time on this area than ever before. Not only that, you are going to have to be very professional about the message you want people to hear, both inside and outside your business. This means that communication – the right type of communication at the right time – is going to assume a much more serious role. This is interesting, because – a few corporations aside – communications has rarely been taken very seriously by management. And this is particularly true of internal communications. As one Swiss based manager told us, 'no one ever made CEO by working in internal communications'.

Well maybe not until now. Having talked with managers in the US and Europe on this issue, our view is that communications, and particularly internal

communications, are going to assume a much more critical role. This means that any firm that takes its reputation, and the long-term maintenance of that reputation, seriously, is going to have to work hard to upgrade its internal communications operation. Much as companies have appointed vice presidents of talent to both seek out and secure the people they need, internal communications professionals will be required to hone the firm's message: a message that will not just help to retain people but attract new talent as well.

Right now, internal communications is not, for the most part, well served with professionals. As a German manager pointed out to us, 'my assistant does the internal communications role on a Friday afternoon, when her work is finished'. Sadly, in too many corporations, that sums it up all too accurately. What we are most certainly going to have to do is massively upgrade the function, staffing it with well-trained communication professionals who can, as one manager put it, 'tell the CEO what's needed and stand up to him or her if necessary'. The problem of course is that there are very few good internal communications people around – it hasn't been seen as a great career step until now – but with this new emphasis on the need to communicate, concisely, clearly and constantly, our view is that this role is going to be a key one in building and maintaining a firm's reputation.

Equally, external communication – specifically about the firm as an employer – is going to need more professionalism. Right now, too many firms leave this to the marketing department and it gets added onto advertising and sponsorship operations. That just won't do in this complex world where new methods of reward, diversity and flexibility will rule. And virtually all of those we interviewed see both internal and external communications as staff roles, not something you can farm out to a public relations firm. Sure you can buy in external specialists to help, but management of reputation is a strategic issue and needs the involvement and support of a senior manager to fully succeed. In our research, we came across a lot of instances where the CEO – especially in firms with high reputations – takes on the role of chief communicator. Interestingly enough, it is in those firms that the CEO also sees himself or herself as the chief human resources officer as well. So, expect communications to assume a far more prominent and higher level role. If you value your talent and want to retain it, as well as attract new employees, it is going to need to be managed – well.

The other issue that has come rapidly to the fore – probably driven by the corporate governance scandals of 2002 is corporate social responsibility (CSR). Again, it would seem that business is going to have little choice but to put this on the agenda and get someone serious and senior to be responsible for it. Cynics point out that CSR is just an attempt for companies to put their house in order before they

are forced to by regulation, but our research shows that the majority of people we discussed this with see it as a worthwhile activity, because it does enhance reputation. What emerging CSR programmes do is formally bring together much of the corporate activity that is already being done under one umbrella. By auditing and assessing activity, companies are better placed to communicate their overall attitudes and activity in areas like the environment, purchasing, third party relationships, charitable support and so on. There has been a massive increase in the number of so-called 'social reports' being developed annually by business and these require the involvement of senior management. As more and more prospective employees seek a detailed background check on prospective employers, CSR communications will assume an ever more vital role in reputation building.

> *I think prospective employees still ask the same questions, they just listen a lot closer to the answers.*
>
> VP HR, Electronics industry.

Finally, corporate governance will continue on the agenda for years to come as a critical issue. Companies have to not just act responsibly, but be seen to be doing so. Our research made it clear that talented individuals are not about to sign up with a new employer unless they are very sure it is squeaky clean from top to bottom. This puts a great deal of pressure onto business and on both internal and external board members. However, responsibility and reputation go hand-in-hand these days and you can expect this to be a very hot agenda item for a long time to come. But sticking with our theme of recruitment, reward and retention, all of these are going to be affected by the reputation for honesty and being seen as a responsible corporate citizen. 'I am amazed about the knowledge prospective employees have about our firm', says a British manager. He adds, 'They have gone to great lengths to check us out and if we don't match up, or cannot answer their concerns, they just won't sign.' In a similar vein, search firms are discovering the same issues with candidates who demand – and get – a 'great deal of detail on just how responsible an employer a company is'.

Case study 1.1

Technitrol – creating a statement of principles

As part of the need to be seen to be responsible, many corporations have written a statement of principles, that essentially lays out what the company stands for in its internal and external relations. One such company, Technitrol, a leading global components supplier has a 13-point Statement of Principles that looks like this:

1. We are a highly ethical company with a strong tradition of complying with all applicable laws in letter and in spirit even when/where others depart. This principle applies to the conduct of all directors, officers, employees and consultants of Technitrol and its business segments anywhere in the world.
2. We employ a global workforce whose background is very diverse. We respect its differences and applaud its positive effects on the company. The diversity of our operations and our employees is a bedrock strength. We are, wherever we operate, a local, global company.
3. We value our customers by understanding their businesses, listening to their needs and building high quality products on time and within an agreed-upon pricing structure.
4. We value and reward professional competence, leadership and every level and teamwork with a capital 'T'.
5. We want to grow with our customers, have a business relationship based on honesty, trust and respect and be their component supplier of choice.
6. We establish financial and non-financial practices competitive with our peer group companies so our employees can do their best work at all times on behalf of our customers.
7. We respect the privacy and innate human dignity of all people. We treat all persons with dignity and respect and endeavour to provide a work environment consistent with this principle. Harassment of any type is inconsistent with this principle and is not tolerated.
8. We (a) ensure that our global operations and all of our products do not harm the environment or endanger the health and safety of our employees, customer or the public and (b) insist on strict compliance with all applicable environmental laws in all countries where we do business. Where reasonably possible, outside of the United States, we apply United States environmental and employee safety standards to our operations.
9. We do not discriminate in the hiring, discharge, compensation, promotion or benefits offered to any employee or applicant on the basis of race, sex, religion, age, disability, sexual orientation or any other basis. We treat all qualified people equally.
10. We conduct our business in compliance with the laws of the United States and other anti-trust and similar laws that apply to our global operations. We will encourage fair competition in the marketplace for our products.
11. We want employees who are honest, trustworthy, hardworking and completely committed to the application of our Statement of Principles and to our success (financial and otherwise) as a business enterprise. An employee who has financial interests in another company or competitor must disclose that potential conflict unless the interest consists of only a minority of nominal ownership of stock in a publicly traded company.
12. Within the context of varied social systems where we do business around the world, we strive to: (a) improve the working lives of our employees, (b) improve the overall lives of

our employees as whole persons, and (c) influence progress in local social conditions whether only in the context of our own operations or, if reasonably possible, more broadly.

13. We prefer to do business with companies, as our agents or our vendors, who endorse Technitrol's Statement of Principles.

EFFECTIVE MANAGEMENT OF EXPECTATIONS

Reporting on our discussions and research on trust earlier, we concluded that it may well be naïve of organizations to believe that you can recreate what you have destroyed. The jury may be out on that, but one thing is very clear from our investigations: if we cannot successfully manage the expectations of our people, we will not be able to operate successfully in the new world of work. As we said earlier, these key human resource issues all overlap, and the effective management of the expectations of our employees is no exception. We need to know – and quickly – just what our employees want, both collectively and individually. What are their needs, their hopes, their aspirations? Where do they see themselves in five years; do we know and can we help them get there?

Today, in 2003, people have many choices, if we cannot help them to harness their energies and engage them in our business, they are going to go elsewhere. Once again this is an item for the strategic agenda and it is going to require time to come up with the right response. But we do need to do it. All of us are required to audit our employees – and ourselves – and begin to track what people expect of us and how we get there. We need to create individual plans, and also remember that not everyone seeks a promotion or more responsibility. Expectations come in many forms and don't just come to a halt at the end of a working day. Expectations go beyond the boundaries of work and if we don't know what our employees aspire to then how can we have meaningful conversations with them.

Time and again in our research, we were told that, 'we must do a better job of engaging our employees. We need to be able to successfully respond to their expectations.' What's worrying is that we didn't see too many organizations doing a great job of it. But, from what we have heard, we are convinced that corporate failure to develop dialogue with employees is going to result in serious, lasting consequences. 'People today expect to be told the truth, they expect to be part of decisions and they want answers when they ask why we are doing something', commented a Paris-based executive. He added, 'If I can't tell them why we are doing something and how it affects them, then I am not doing my job.' Managing expectations effectively is a great motivator, it just has to be done in a more

organized and formal fashion. Look for this to take precedence in smart-thinking businesses in the coming years.

> *Prospective employees know a whole lot more about your business than they ever did. They are going to ask you, 'Why did these people leave?', 'What are your plans for this division?' Five years ago, no one would ever have asked me these types of questions.*
>
> VP Operations, Automotive industry.

NEW ORGANIZATIONAL STRUCTURES

When the hierarchical pyramids of command and control-style management collapsed into the flat structures of the 1990s (with the 'help' of a million or so consultants and external advisers) we hailed a new organizational era. Looking around us today in 2003, what we see is not so much any new organizational structures, but just the same businesses, with the same departments and the same command and control style in lots of cases. What happened? Our discussions indicate that three years of recession have not been at all good for new-style, hierarchy-free business. Essentially, as the economy slumped, the 'numbers' men and women took over the levers of power and that is still the case in much of corporate America and Europe. But our concern is not what is happening now, it is about what happens next.

There is a lot of evidence out there right now that points to some type of revolution in how our organizations will function in the future and how they will be staffed. Most of this is not predicated on it being a 'nice thing to do', but on the simple fact that businesses are highly complex, technologically advanced and global in their scope in one form or another. While we don't advocate the wholesale removal of marketing, finance, human resources and other titles, we do see major change on the horizon, driven by necessity not fashion.

Our view, borne out by our interviews across Europe and the US, is that business has changed so much in recent times that there are new imperatives that drive our firms. These imperatives demand that we create new positions of responsibility and authority that have not existed before. We are not sure what their titles will be or just how wide their responsibilities, but we are certain that we are on the verge of a new organizational structure that will require totally new jobs to achieve its goals.

We have touched on many of these responsibilities in discussing the issues like reward and reputation, but there are considerably more. Based on our own investigation and the views of our interviewees, here are some of the new jobs that the twenty-first-century business is going to need, and why they will need them.

Corporate integrationists

These professionals are already a hot-ticket item for many corporations. Why? Well there are not many truly professional, skilled integrationists around and they are in very short supply. Why do companies need them? What we discovered in our research was that following the acquisition craze of the 1990s many businesses never entirely got to grips with their new prizes. In case after case, they never really got around to fully integrating the companies they had bought, into one homogenous whole. Now, pushed against a wall by recession and tumbling sales, they have an urgent need to make cost savings and 'manage the hell' out of their total operation. In doing this the skills of a corporate integrationist are paramount. They are able to look across management disciplines to see how the overall business could look by massaging all the parts in the right way. While a lot of this is based on getting the right sort of people equations in place and knocking down the silos of stand-alone corporate inefficiency, it is also about helping others in the business leverage savings and opportunities (e.g. better logistics, brand development, R&D sharing, bulk purchasing and so on). Whether they are called corporate integrationists or not, senior managers with these skills are deeply involved in redrawing the future of a host of corporations around the globe. Expect them to stay premium priced and in ever shorter supply.

Logistic gurus

There is no doubt that logistics (and that includes purchasing) is going to have a long-lasting influence on our businesses. Highly experienced logistics professionals are already in great demand; even to the extent of regularly crossing industry boundaries. The simple reason for their popularity is that they can *make* the difference between profit and loss throughout a business. In our view, logistics in one form or another, is going to be one of the key drivers of the next economic cycle. Whether it is organizing global purchasing opportunities, or delivering just-in-time solutions for manufacturing or customers, the logistics professional will become a major part of any corporation that makes, moves and markets stuff.

And as manufacturing gets moved away to second and third tier suppliers, their role will become ever more important.

Within the logistics boundary are other key players. Number one is the *outsourcer*. As we have been told, outsourcing has now become one of the main tasks of industries that used to manufacture everything themselves. But as we know, outsourcing now covers everything from security and office cleaning, to manufacture, distribution, marketing, human resources and after-sales service. Many managers believe that you can outsource anything if the price is right. There is little doubt, from what we have learned in our interviews, that outsourcing is getting more and more prevalent. Not only that, it is finally being recognized as a job function in its own right. If you consider that up until recently, outsourcing has been done by managers in different departments with no links to one another (HR outsources pensions and salary administration; manufacturing outsources whole lines of products; IT outsources the entire management information system), then you can visualize what would happen if your chief outsourcing executive, started to begin to put a lot of this together. Our view, again based on what the real world tells us, is that outsourcing professionals are going to be key. They may carry a logistics title, they may even be those integrationists. Whatever the job title, they will begin to revolutionize how we operate our businesses.

Multi-tasking general managers

The first thing to say about these people is that they are not a new talent discovery at all, they have always been there. It is just that no one has looked very closely at them for some time. Now they are back in fashion. Why? Consider this. You are opening an operation in China. What do you do, send a newly minted MBA? Of course not. What you need is a seasoned management professional who knows enough about your business, your products, people, finance, manufacturing to get the job done: the sort of person who hits the ground running and just keeps on running without calling head office all the time. Well the good news is that they are still out there. The bad news is that a lot of them are needed as we expand our businesses and so they are also going to be in short supply.

Senior-level people developers

Coaching and mentoring may be popular right now, but we are not talking about that. What we are talking about is the ravenous need by corporations to make their best people better. Take your top 10 per cent and make them 10 per cent

more productive and you have a winning concept on your hands. As several people we interviewed put it, 'it doesn't matter about the other 90 per cent, they'll do their jobs one way or another, *but* if we can get that top 10 per cent of our people doing 5, 10 or 20 per cent better then we are breaking through all sorts of barriers'. To do that corporations are going to need a whole new breed of development specialists who understand how to make the already exceptional even more so. Companies are already bringing these people on board (some firm's use outside help, others say that the confidentiality aspects preclude doing that) and they are tasked with one simple goal, 'get the people we have identified as tomorrow's key players into the best shape you can'. Look for this crusade-to-be-better to continue.

Security hot-shots

Post 9/11 corporations the world over went hunting for talent that could ring-fence their business. Now in 2003 they have wised-up a little and stopped pounding the panic button. That means that they have now taken a measured, sober look at their needs, equating the search for the right talent to where they operate (geographically) and how their organization functions. With that solved, most companies have concluded that they don't need Rambo-style look-alikes who can physically defend them. The real threat comes much more from computer-related crimes, most of which (due to deep corporate embarrassment) never get reported. However, all the organizations we have talked to have in one way or another taken on board that an external hacker (even those just bent on simple-minded mischief) can seriously screw up their operations. So security takes on a bigger role in these new business models as well.

Talent managers

We've talked about this earlier, but talent managers are going to feature large in the corporations of tomorrow, for the simple reason that we will not be able to sate our appetite for good people. This may appear a not very useful thought in the midst of downturns and downsizing, but we will very quickly run out of people come any kind of upswing: Europe, the US and Asia are all vulnerable to this. Our view is that smart corporations have already done their homework, done their audits and know two things: (1) who they want to keep whatever the cost and (2) who they want to buy when they become available or go job hunting. We will all need talent managers in one form or another, be they former human

resources professionals or totally new recruits into the business world. We can expect the best to be – as usual – in short supply.

Communication professionals

As we already indicated earlier in this chapter, communications, both internal and external, will take on a bigger and more overt roll in all of our businesses. To make that happen we are going to have to find, train and develop a whole new set of professional skills (because there aren't many around right now). We would expect to see this as a new, exciting career path (that can well include responsibilities for shareholder relations and corporate social responsibility). Right now – like talent managers, there are not a lot of these professionals around, but expect the ranks to grow as firms rush to be more transparent and more accountable, from the point of view that it's just good for business to do it that way.

So this is the new world of work that is waiting to happen. Our feeling is that it is going to be challenging, exciting and rewarding for those prepared to go the distance. What we also have to be mindful of though is that this *is* a new world of work and some won't want to make the journey.

There is no doubt that there is an emerging trend for people to opt out of the business world and look for other life solutions. As many of our interviewees told us, this is an issue that crosses generations and industries and could cause a severe talent drought if it continues. It was roundly summed up by one of the smartest human resource thinkers in the US when he told us, 'I'm not saying that this is a real trend yet, but I have now had this conversation 30 or 40 times in the past twelve months.' He continues, 'it goes like this: "you know I have been really happy here for the last ten years, but I have talked things over with my wife and I am going off to be a teacher in Indiana". That is a conversation I am having on an increasing basis. These are not talentless losers, these are people we'd like to keep, but they are taking a different road and opting for a less stressful, less money-driven lifestyle.'

And this isn't a post 9/11 US phenomenon either. It is happening in Europe too. British, Dutch and German managers are bailing out too and heading for less stressful, but possibly more psychologically rewarding experiences in rural France. As in the US they are not rich – in many cases their stock portfolio is underwater. They have just taking the decision to reassess their lives. As a banker in the city of London says, 'every month we lose one or two, our concern is when does the trickle become a flood'. Right now for every corporate escapee, there is a job-seeker fairly eager (if only to make ends meet) to take the job. But come that

upturn, who knows what will happen. The view of those we interviewed is very straightforward on both sides of the Atlantic: the smart managers are worried and they know that problems are going to come along that they will have to fix.

The really smart companies have used this economic downturn to good purpose and know what their organizations need to be in the future and they also know who they will need to make that happen. The only real concern is, will they have enough talent to make it all happen?

Case study 1.2

Checking out the scandals

The Conference Boards Commission on Public Trust and Private Enterprise was formed to address the circumstances which led to recent corporate scandals. In its report, it describes executive compensation as the 'Perfect Storm'.

According to the report, the Federal Reserve Chairman, Alan Greenspan described excessive executive compensation of the past decade as 'excessive greed'. And the Commission itself said it believed that there had been a 'Perfect Storm', a confluence of events in the compensation area which created an environment ripe for abuse.

Among the Conference Board Commission's findings were:

- The use of stock options and other equity-based incentives resulted in an enormous incentive to manage companies for short-term stock price gains.
- Boards of directors became lax in performing their historical duty to monitor compensation.
- This unprecedented bull market led to massive unanticipated gains from options unrelated to management's operating performance.

And then CEOs and others wonder why the trust in business has gone.

2

Making the difference in our businesses

INTRODUCTION

In Chapter 1, we talked about the trends and issues that are going to seriously affect how we work in the future, but that's not all we are going to have to contend with in the changed corporate landscape we will have to operate in. According to our research there are a lot of people development actions that we are going to have to take very seriously if we are to be competitive in the new world of work. In conversations with senior managers on both sides of the Atlantic it became clear that there were recurring concerns about how we will manage the people in our organizations come the upturn.

The most frequently mentioned people-issues were:

- Engage your employees
- Knock over those hierarchical silos – again!
- Learn how to better manage alliances
- Manage people who have choices and are seeking a true work–life balance
- Understand and manage the demographic barriers
- Make it easier for people to do their jobs.

ENGAGE YOUR EMPLOYEES

There are strong feelings out there in mainstream corporate Europe and the US that with trust firmly scratched off the employee/employer contract there needs to be something to put in its place, that will engage employees. For many, this seems to be based around the concept of a competency-based structure where people see their value increase as they develop skills. 'What we are trying to do', said a Paris based HR manager, 'is to make every employee know why they are coming to work, what we will give them in terms of tools to do and develop their jobs and what that means in terms of reward.' Their view, and one held by many others, is that by spelling out what the company is prepared to do, you automatically give the employees a sense of individual and mutual purpose.

This would seem the sensible option taken by people across a broad base of industries. 'I am certain', says a Wall Street banker, 'that we have to keep our people motivated and I am personally more concerned about the broad population and how to make them feel wanted by us. That for me is going to be the biggest challenge.' He adds, 'We need to keep our workforces engaged to give them a real, honest vision of the future and I don't think we have too much time to do this.'

Others concur, that engaging people is a paramount objective. 'Look what we did as we exited the 1990s', commented a New York based manager, 'we were shoving newly-minted MBAs into management slots without any idea of what we, or they, were doing there. They didn't get the people thing at all. We were buying in people with no management experience and zero people skills, and just look where all that got us.'

> *Think about our future task this way. If you were in a room and no one knew who you were, would they follow you? Or are they going to say, 'oh no, is this really* the *leader? Get me out of here!'*
>
> VP HR, Financial Services industry.

'Every company should be closely auditing its workforce right now', says a general manager of a major engineering unit in Frankfurt, 'because, if we are honest with ourselves, we don't know what our people will do come the upturn. What we do know is that if we haven't got a very good story to give them they won't stay.' They won't have to, the shortages will be immense once business picks up. A mid-Western engineer agrees, 'The last decade has probably destroyed manufacturing for America', he says, 'everyone went for an MBA and became a bond trader, so there won't be any mid-level engineers to take over.' They continue, 'Remember the good old days? You got into senior management at the 40 to 55 period and you hadn't been spoiled beforehand.'

So what are corporations doing about it? Keeping people engaged and hoping that their reputation as an employer who treated its people fairly – even those they let go – in the down times will carry them through and hope they don't leak too much talent when they least need to. From our discussions, that seems about all they can do. One high-technology industry manager summed it up by saying, 'we won't know how well we've done our job of retaining people until we find out how many go and how many leave. I'd like to think we've done a very good job, trouble is I won't find out until it's too late.'

KNOCK OVER THOSE HIERARCHICAL SILOS – AGAIN!

Knocking down silos was a very popular corporate mission in the late 1990s. According to those we spoke to, these recent parlous times have seen them being built back up again. 'When the going gets tough, the smart managers circle the wagons and wait it out', says a transportation industry veteran, 'They know one

of the true adages of business, that knowledge is power, and that if they keep their bit of the business in shape and make the numbers everyone will turn a blind eye to the rogue state you have just created.'

But come better times, everyone will be talking about making synergies across divisions, sharing resources and so on. It will be time to dismantle the defensive silos once more. 'A lot of seasoned managers know only too well that they can build their own castle, pull up the drawbridge and get away with it while everyone is looking the other way and fretting over tumbling sales figures', says a London-based management consultant. 'Especially if they are turning in results, no one is going to mess them around. Unfortunately, long term it isn't a very efficient way to operate, but there are a lot of feudal lords out there having one last crack at power.' Others report that they have seen a rash of newly appointed country managers taking over the running of Europe-wide businesses in what one executive described as a 'return to the 1960s business model'.

But it does look as though this type of grab-it-while-you-can behaviour will be short-lived. Those silos are going to have to come down – again.

Feed the machine

After years of writing about organizational issues, I thought I had got them all worked out: I was wrong! In the early days of interviewing for this book I had a meeting with a young, dynamic woman who was leaving her employer of almost a decade for one simple reason. Her next move, she had been told, needed to be to the US and their headquarters. Although marked down as a high-potential she decided to say no to the move. The upshot was that she was going nowhere in the business. Eventually, thanks to a kind headhunter, she was offered a job in another industry in a very high profile job.

Talking this over some months later with a group in New York, I mentioned how stupid some firms can be to invest all that time and money in a high potential and then to let them go like that. Several people at the table shook their heads and laughed. 'Mike, it doesn't work that way', they said, 'she was expendable, she was a human sacrifice'.

'I don't get it', I said, 'what do you mean?'

'She refused to go to HQ and eventually she lost her job, right? Well that sent a message to the other 300 high potentials, who *are* going to go and do their time in the US. That company is a fine-honed machine, where cogs that

continued...

step ever so slightly out of line get crushed very quickly. You cannot afford that kind of dissention. The message is clear and everyone else has, by now, understood it. Sacrificing one person and the cost of their development means nothing if everyone else understands the message it sends.'

LEARN HOW TO BETTER MANAGE ALLIANCES

The shell-shocked veterans of economic recession are going to be very cautious about staffing up too fast. So it seems clear that outsourcing work and the establishment of temporary or permanent alliances will become much more prevalent. This will create a real challenge for companies as there will be a huge need for 'those able to manage remote matrix resources, where talent could be under contract or belong to someone else', notes a US engineer. 'In this case people who have negotiation and persuasion skills are going to be at a premium.'

The view of the market is that outsourcing and value-chain management will become major trends that will quickly change the way we run our businesses. 'If we outsource our manufacturing and logistics', says one French manager, 'then we need to make sure we have the skills in value-chain engineering to do this effectively. Right now there are not that many people training up for this, so there will certainly be a talent shortage.' A US-based manager agrees, 'What worries me is that I haven't heard of any business school teaching outsourcing or value-chain engineering, but we need these people now.'

Whatever you do, don't ever think that HR understands the new generation – it doesn't ... and they don't understand us either. So it is going to take a lot – an awful lot – to get these people on board, never mind keep them.

VP HR, Pharmaceuticals industry.

All these new-world-of-work jobs will require the successful management and development of alliances – without that they won't work, so the expectation is of a growing talent famine in this area in the next two years. 'Certainly this is the way the world is moving', suggests a Brussels-based manager. 'Look at the pharmaceuticals industry, it markets and does R&D, the rest it outsources to people who do it better and cheaper.'

Adds another, 'We will be putting a real premium onto the heads of those who can sell their ideas to a diverse group of people who don't have to say "yes". But I am concerned about coming shortages, so I think what all of us in business should be doing right now is working out how to do it better with the people we already have.'

MANAGE PEOPLE WHO HAVE CHOICES AND ARE SEEKING A TRUE WORK–LIFE BALANCE

We covered some of the work-life balance (WLB) issues in Chapter 1, but it is useful to put them on the agenda again. Despite what some people seem to think (that there is no room for WLB in a recessionary period), all our research points to the simple fact that WLB is a major factor in determining choice of career and will continue to be so. In our individual and group interviews, virtually everyone at some point raised the WLB issue: usually in an attempt to find out what others are doing about it. But our view is that, while not every organization has a formal WLB policy, everyone has been affected by the issue and expects to be affected further in the years to come. There is no doubt that employees (even engaged employees) are baling out for other, less stressful or more meaningful lives. And this is happening in the US and in Europe too. What this means is that business is facing a recruitment crisis of unprecedented proportions. We already know that the demographics of tumbling birth rates are reducing the available workforce, but what we are not too sure about (because we seem to lack hard data on it) is just how many people are turning their backs on a career in mainstream business. What this research has made us sure of though, is that people today have more choices in what they can do as a career than even a decade ago, and with the reputation of business at an all-time low, we are not picking up as many people as we might have.

Not only are people making alternative lifestyle choices at the beginning of their career, they are beginning to examine their chosen career in their middle age as well. We have all heard the stories of the so-called careerist who take one long, wet commute too many, or had a health shock that woke him or her up.

Additionally, in both Europe and the US many managers are inheriting significant wealth from their parents and finding middle-aged financial independence. Why work when you don't have to? Or, at least, why work so hard?

There is no doubt among the people we talked to for this book that possibly the greatest challenge for business for the next ten years will be to hire and hold people for the very simple reason that in our twenty-first-century society we have created multiple-choice options for everyone. This isn't one of those people problems for the back burner, this is a volcano that threatens to explode our cosy business world. We already saw what a shortage of talent can do to stunt our growth in the late 1990s, now it is going to happen again. Except this time some of the players don't want to be on our team anymore.

> *Europe* invests *in people, the US sees people as a* cost. *I would hope to see a change in this attitude.*
>
> General manager, Engineering industry.

While it may be tough to engage people who don't trust you, that is going to look easy beside the fact that they don't even get a chance not to trust you because they never show up at your door in the first place. Neither do our experts who are trying to work on these issues see the concept of throwing money at it being much of a help either. We are going to have to learn to work this through by dealing with people in a totally different way.

In that we will have to, however reluctantly, accept that:

- Home or remote working must be an option on offer for all employees.
- Trade-ins of salary for time off must be an option too.
- Flexible work hours and work weeks and going to be the norm.
- Maternity leave, should include a permanent home-work solution if required.
- Sabbaticals are going to be part of the employee package.
- Some of our employees are going to get rich. So how can we continue to work with them?
- Some of our employees want to go part time. How can we make that happen so it works for both sides?
- Many of our 'employees' will be contract workers. How do we manage them effectively?
- People get bored with their jobs. So find ways to get them to rotate their jobs, add new elements to them or just migrate elsewhere for a while.

If we haven't got answers, policies and procedures for all of this, then we will be in poor shape to get any value from the new world of work. It isn't a possibility, it

is happening right now inside *your* business. It doesn't have to be negative, it can, if worked out, be a powerful, and positive opportunity to really re-engage people.

UNDERSTAND AND MANAGE THE DEMOGRAPHIC BARRIERS

We have already touched on this in the section above, but understanding the shifting sands of demographics and how they will affect the workplace is going to be key to corporate survival. Most certainly, it is going to be the key to ensuring we have a healthy supply of talented employees. From what we have already learned in our research, we suspect that organizations are beginning to understand that – recessions apart – there is going to be a dwindling supply of people to help them meet their future growth targets. More importantly, we suspect they sort of know it but aren't doing that much about it.

Our view is that this (like WLB) has to get onto the strategic corporate agenda – *soon*. What our investigations have shown, is that not enough organizations are really that concerned – yet – about where tomorrow's talent will come from. Mired in recession and shedding employees, it is all too easy to look the other way. But there is little doubt that come that upturn people are going to be in short supply.

And we are talking across the board, across geographies and across (possibly most importantly) age groups. Let's take a look at those groupings and consider what business *should* be doing *now*.

An entrepreneurial explosion?

Talking to senior managers on both sides of the Atlantic, there is a definite feeling that we may be on the verge of an explosion of entrepreneurial initiatives. This is predicated on the fact that many bright, energetic young managers have been laid off in recent months and they are out there tinkering with all sorts of new ideas. One example that proves the point and seems to have gone unreported so far is in California, home of high technology. There in 2002 alone there were more than 80 start-ups using advanced microchip technologies, which are now (especially for those buying second-hand, refurbished machinery) relatively inexpensive. Our intelligence gathering shows that this type of tech-driven start-up activity is also happening in Europe to a certain extent as smart engineers and other managers decide to take a entrepreneurial chance rather than just make the rounds like other job-seekers. From this activity, we can expect a rash of new products and processes.

- *The under 25s:* Our thought, based on our interviews, is that while groups of graduates who a decade ago would have marched willingly into the corporate world are taking other options. As we said, there are a lot of choices today that don't include private enterprise, are virtually the same in monetary reward and carry both greater job satisfaction and greater job security. This group is the first hurdle. If we cannot convince a good percentage of them to come over to our side we are going to have serious problems to get sufficient talent into our organizations to make them work. Much of that is going to come from the overall perception of business that these people have. Right now it is a lousy perception. Our view is that individual companies can, and will, by their actions, get new graduates to join them, but none of us should take this as a given. A dedicated programme devoted to getting your firm in front of potential employees needs to be in place and needs to be monitored closely.
- *The over 55s:* If anyone is taking the money and running it is this group. But we made them do it, we forced them to it by short-sighted policies. Now we are – belatedly – realizing that we need these people – badly. They are the 'history' and the 'knowledge' of our business and we have so far just let them go. A few smart organizations are saying, 'we can't do that, we our throwing our knowledge away'.

  Believe us, it doesn't matter if these people want to work just one day a week, find a way to keep them. If they want to retire to Florida or southern Spain, give them a lap-top and an e-mail address and plug into what they know. In most cases they'll appreciate it and you'll make money. Any CEO who doesn't have 'saving the 55+ people's knowledge, contacts and experience' on his agenda should be fired.

Can you still sprint?

One of the issues that is concerning managers is what sort of role do you give to the over-50s in your business? This question has become a lot more critical in the past few years as many older managers have found themselves faced with stock and pension pay-out concerns: meaning that they have little choice but to continue to work. One of the potential problems is the pure psychology of the issue. If you had planned to retire at 55 and find you can't, can you get back into the race again? When you look around at most businesses today everyone is sprinting for most of the time. So what managers need to do is ask the question, 'if you have mentally slowed down to a jog, because your plans were to quit in a couple of years, can you begin to sprint again?'

Continued...

The view of most of the managers we talked to was, 'no you can't'. Once you are off the treadmill it is very hard to get back on and even harder to maintain the pace. Said one New York-based manager, 'What we have to do is find ways to use older executives, probably in mentoring roles, when they can use their knowledge for the good of the next generation.'

The other issue here is making sure that younger executives don't get frustrated by the log-jam of ageing managers at the top of the business. Noted a telecommunication manager from Atlanta, 'We have got to get our organizations set up so that older managers can stand aside and let younger managers have a go too.' He added, 'We say we want these people for their experience and knowledge, well, we have to create the conditions so that they can do that without hindering the next generation.'

Did we miss some people? Yes we did. There's a whole two decades we have not included, the 35 to 55s. Right now, they (the ones still in employment) are the expert talent, the specialist talent that keeps business running. But they are possibly the most vulnerable to the concept of bailing out. Do you know who they are; do you have a plan to retain the ones you need, even if it takes a *lot* of flexibility in the employment offer? Worse than that, the pool we can draw from to make good leaders has been diminished. As we observed earlier, many ran off to be bankers and traders and never made it back, others were discouraged from taking up an engineering career. Most of all the rest were given specialists assignments and drilled down on those. The end result is that we killed off a huge portion of our leadership potential by not fashioning them into leadership material. Now we will reap the sad harvest of having few people with the people skills and the leadership skills to make the difference we need.

The average manager in Europe is still totally ill-equipped to find a new job on their own, they need help: a lot of it.

CEO, Outplacement industry.

MAKE IT EASIER FOR PEOPLE TO DO THEIR JOBS

During our investigations, we were lucky enough to meet some truly honest managers that were only too pleased (well it was off the record) to tell us where

they had gone wrong. One of the recurring themes that came up was, 'we realized we were actually making it hard for our people – our employees – to do their jobs'.

Several companies told us that, alarmed at people leaving, they had instituted a far more rigorous system of exit interviews. What these proved was astounding. As one New York-based manager admitted, 'we found that the reason people were quitting was because they had got bored with what they were doing and felt like a change'. He continued, 'the bucket of cold water in the face came, when we realized that in 70 per cent of the cases the job they had gone to do, was actually available and open in our own firm'.

Getting it wrong that badly has spurred many into action and the results have made interesting reading. Indeed one of the major accounting firms introduced an electronic job vacancy board for internal openings and had the salutatory experience of more than 30 per cent of the staff applying for other jobs within the first 48 hours. As they commented, 'you begin to realize that you haven't really been doing very much to either motivate or retain your talent when you get a result like that'.

There was also a strong feeling that technology – office technology – had done a wonderful job in keeping people apart, 'When staff in open-plan offices e-mail each other instead of talking face-to-face you have the recipe for serious problems', observed one financial services manager. 'The problem with e-mail is that it totally stunts creativity and curiosity. We ask for information, we get a response, and that's that. There is none of that, "I was thinking, couldn't we do this in a different way?", type of thinking.'

Again, it seems a simple step to get people concerned about making it easy for staff to do their jobs. In reality we don't. In fact many of us just build up barriers to letting people communicate and learn from one another. When frustration boils over people leave or decide that they will just live in their own safe little community. That is not how to build a business – but we manage to do these things to people every day.

High flyers wanted

How much autonomy should managers have? This story has been told many times but asking 250 HR managers the question shows we still have some way to go in wielding total power.

You are on a plane and you sit next to a person who you realize is the greatest manager you have ever met. You instinctively know that this person

Continued...

is totally the right person for your business. So do you, as the head of HR, have the power to make them an offer on the spot?

Here's how 250 managers answered?[1]

Yes	28.6 per cent
No	64.7 per cent
Not stated	6.7 per cent

Our thought is that it should be a corporate imperative to know why people quit and it should also be on the agenda to find out just how frustrated people are with their lack of ability to progress or change.

As one Philadelphia-based manager told us, 'These days no one is going to wait five years for a change, they either grow or go. I don't mean huge promotions, I just mean some variety in what they do. If we can't provide that and monitor closely what we are doing we cannot be surprised if we lose people.'

I would honestly say that in my career 80 per cent of the top managers I have recruited don't have the basic values you need to run a business.

VP HR, Financial services industry.

Said another, 'I had a very sobering experience last week. I had an exit interview with a bright, young individual who when asked why she was leaving told me, "my presence here made no difference at all. When I leave, it will be like pulling my finger out of a glass of water, I'll leave no trace behind me".' He went on, 'I was ashamed by that and I realized, possibly for the first time, that employees today have less tolerance for not being excited and engaged than previous generations. I realized if we didn't change our ideas, we would never, ever hold onto the people we need.'

Case study 2.1

Nestlé – key concepts of a corporation

Food giant Nestlé has long been regarded as an innovative employer of people. Recently, under the title of 'Key Concepts', they sought to define the way people in the organization should act and interact. Their corporate view of the business of tomorrow provides an interesting blueprint. Here is what they say are the key concepts on which the business is based.

1 HR managers quizzed in a Richmond Events poll at their Human Resources Conference in October 2002.

- *Network:* Hierarchy is progressively referred to as a manager's capability to influence action taken by his peers and subordinates. Operating as a 'hub', the manager concentrates on leading, providing focus and enhancing cooperation.
- *Insight:* Experience is not enough. Experience needs to be transformed into insight. Insight reflects the capacity to link the past with the future by transforming knowledge into actions and results.
- *Alignment:* Result orientation provides better focus than command, which it replaces progressively. The issue is to ensure proper alignment of action, rather than merely obeying orders.
- *Co-operating:* The skills needed for work and learning include self-direction together with a strong willingness to support others, to work in multi-skilled teams, to co-operate rather than compete. More emphasis on building trust enhances resolving conflicts and solving problems. Competition should be geared externally on competitors.
- *Initiative:* Initiatives are enhanced when people find ways to maintain a strong feeling of self-efficacy and control over their lives in the face of challenges. Reducing that feeling will impact negatively on the capacity to take initiatives.
- *Cross-border/functional:* The traditional organization chart does not any longer reflect the need of cross-functional or cross-national co-operation. Flexible co-operation patterns provide a better combination of skills and a better design of focus.

What we have discussed in this chapter isn't complex, it *is* easy to do if we apply ourselves. Our view – and the view of all of corporate America and Europe that we talked to is, 'we have to get better at this basic stuff'. So why can't we? Why can we admit it in interviews and not do it in practice? Because it is obvious we are still getting the basics wrong in very many cases.

> *You know the secretaries now steal the pens and pencils. They think they are entitled, because the boss 'stole' millions. How do I argue with that?*
>
> VP HR, Insurance industry.

Take on one thing. Employees today are *not* like they used to be. They demand open, honest and timely communication. They want to know that their job counts and they want the organization to stop putting roadblocks in the way of their job. Sit back and think about it. We are certain you can think of better ways to motivate your people. Just make a start tomorrow before it is too late.

3

What's going to stay wrong?

INTRODUCTION

There is a terrible tendency when involved in a series of interviews about business to concentrate on the bad things that are happening, rather than looking at the more positive aspects. But the truth is that there has been such a great deal of bad press about business that it is difficult to ignore it. On that basis, we thought the best way to look at the doom and gloom scenarios for business was to put them all into one chapter, so that if you don't want to be depressed further you don't need to read it.

Based on our interviews, we have to report that we think there are a whole host of issues around big business that won't get any better any time soon. These include:

- Wall Street
- CEO tenure
- CEO choice
- The hire and fire society
- Mergers and acquisitions
- Human resources.

WALL STREET

It is a plain fact that much of what has gone wrong with private enterprise in the past decade or so can be laid firmly at Wall Street's door (other financial centres can be blamed for copy cat tactics). By that we mean that their ability to embrace or reject corporate heads, create huge enthusiasms and then pull rugs out from under people has assumed fairly epic proportions. As several people we interviewed pointed out, it wasn't that long ago that asset strippers like Al 'Chainsaw' Dunlap were held up as the model we should all be following. Then we were bullied into believing that dot.coms and telecommunications were the next revolution and then Bernie Ebbers and a cast of greedy look-alikes were the saviours of corporate America. All this has happened in a fairly short space of time and despite these corporate governance scandals there seems no reason for the same thing not to happen again. 'Wall Street exists to encourage this kind of bad behaviour', says one financial services executive. He adds, 'sadly, of course the people running the companies get to believe it too. Think of it this way, "If you have one tenth of your income in salary and the rest is in stock, you sort of lose track of what you have been hired for in the first place."'

CEO TENURE

Throughout the past 30 years the average tenure of CEOs has been getting shorter and shorter. While there are some firms that seem to keep people at the top for a long time (something that seems to link strongly with perceived corporate reputation), there is little sign that this state of affairs is going to change much.

CEOs are increasingly vulnerable to the pressures of Wall Street and their institutional investors and no one we interviewed thought that this would change that much. As we, hopefully, come back from the economic downturn, there will still be huge pressures on CEOs in both the US and Europe to perform, so there is little doubt that there are going to be some new victims along the way.

> *We have a long-tenured top management team who have been in the foxhole together and survived. We think this sends a good message.*
>
> General manager, Oil and gas industry.

According to one study:[1] from 1995 to 2001:

- Turnover of the CEOs of major corporation increased by 53 per cent.
- The number of CEOs departing because of the company's poor financial performance increased by 130 per cent.
- The average tenure of CEOs declined from 9.5 years to 7.3 years.

Interestingly enough, during our research we did have some conversations about which corporations were the best run. Probably number one on everyone's list was Wal-Mart, that just seems to go on its own way. As one manager commented, 'it is a 30-year-old business model but it works. It certainly doesn't look like star material, it is in-bred, but very operationally focused. Possibly best of all is that no one at Wal-Mart gives a damn about what anyone else says about them, they just get on with it.'

Other companies – US in the main – that come in for constant praise are Coca-Cola and Pepsi-Cola that have both stuck to what they know best; Pfizer gets special praise as does Anhauser-Busch. On the technological side, all praise Intel, with Cisco Systems and Oracle as runners up. The best non-US performer, and constantly singled out is Diageo. All of these garner praise for sticking to what they know well and just getting better at it all the time.

---

1 Hamilton (2002) *Why CEOs Fall: The causes and consequences of turnover at the top.* Booz Allen: *Wall Street Journal*, 18 September.

CEO CHOICE

The other issue that goes hand-in-hand with CEO tenure is choice. Too many companies don't seem to get it at all right first or even second time. When you look at the turnover and poor performances being put in by some CEOs you have to question who put them there in the first place. As one manager said, 'What we want are not stars, but people who can deliver consistency and growth.' He added, 'And we don't want them to be too smart either. Any CEO with an IQ of over 115 and you've got trouble. You don't want a CEO who's too bright – they are dangerous. You want a guy who will run the business consistently.'

Trouble is that for a whole swathe of benighted corporations that hasn't happened. The only consistency has been failure to do the job and getting paid a great deal for that failure. Time after time what we have seen is a completely unsuited manager being catapulted into the CEO slot. 'The message that this sends to the ground troops', says a Swiss banker, 'is that no one cares and no one has a clue how to run this place. Then they want people to stop worrying and become productive again.'

> *We are working overtime to fill up the goodwill jar before the upturn, right now it looks a little short of cookies.*
>
> VP HR, Financial services industry.

Help! My CEO's crazy!

During our US interviews we were struck by the number of times senior managers – specifically those with HR responsibilities – said that they had suffered major disputes with their CEO. Explained one, 'When I first started in HR, there was a strong sense of HR's role as balancing the needs of top management and the employees: we were the conscience of the business, the go-between.' They went on, 'Today that role has changed markedly. Today HR have to be fully aligned with the CEO, and that can lead to conflict.'

Added another executive, 'I see an increasing prevalence for "in-your-face" management. I have a very strong sense (not just in my own firm) that what comes from the CEO is in the style of the school-yard bully. I talk to colleagues and they get a lot of this too.' He concluded, 'I think the pressure to perform has gone beyond normal levels and quite honestly I believe that a lot of CEO are unhealthy, sick people and it become more and more pronounced as they hit the skids.'

HIRE AND FIRE SOCIETY

Evidence garnered over the past 18 months makes it all too clear that whatever might have been thought to the contrary, we are still a hire and fire society. Asking senior managers in Europe and the US what they had learned from the recession the answer was 'not much at all'. Asked what they will do when the economy picks up again and they need to hire more people, one explained, 'We'll do what we do every time, throw money at it. The market will improve, there will be a shortage of people and we will once again pay through the nose, until the economy downturns again.' This it would seem is the vicious economic cycle that big business seems quite prepared to go through every decade or so, because it is so much easier than trying to hold on to people.

Indeed employees think that too. A poll in 2002[2] noted that 60 per cent of the respondents said employers fell short in 'showing concern for employees, not just for the financial bottom-line' and 57 per cent said employers fell short in 'being loyal to long-term employees'.

However, there has been one development that we picked up on both in Europe and the US, which we think may well have a significant affect on the next round of recruitment. We think that there is a growing trend for companies to settle on a core group of workers – who they will maintain as employees through good times and bad. When good times come they will be much more likely to use interim workers or short-term contract hire. If this happens – and there is a good body of evidence to suggest that it is already taking place in some industries – we will see the creation of a two-tier employment model; where there is a core cadre of well-paid, well-looked-after employees, supported by a shifting population of outworkers. Rather than being seen as the creation of some type of corporate underclass, many managers say that this style of work will tap into the needs of many, who don't want a permanent career placement or to work 12 months out of the year. However, it is going to be interesting to see how this develops in the years ahead and whether these workers do get rewarded fully for their labours.

MERGERS AND ACQUISITIONS

Despite all that has been researched and written about mergers and acquisitions, companies still make this one of the most unhealthy of all corporate activities.

2 Peter D. Hart research of 900 US employees, August 2002.

As part of the research process we interviewed a cross-section of senior human resource professionals in Europe and the US who had all recently experienced a merger situation (either as acquirer or acquired). From those interviews we distilled the following critical HR-related factors[3] that *do* need to be taken into account. Rather than create a catalogue of disaster, we have suggested some ways to get the people agenda in a merger on the front page as quickly as possible.

- Speed is the most mentioned factor by everyone interviewed, topping all other concerns. All HR-related issues should move as fast as possible: rapid communication, speedy integration of systems, quick decisions on staffing levels. In the early days the difference between a good merger experience and a bad one can come down to nothing less than 'impeccable timing'.
- The first 100 days set the scene for evermore. You have to establish everything you are going to do with the people in the business well within that time-frame.
- One way to avoid instant culture clash is to show from the outset respect for the acquired organization's capabilities. For the company as a whole it can mean the addition of another talent pool, and should be seen in this light: a truly positive spin. If this talent is of a different nature than the existing pool it can be of great benefit to the sustainability of the merger and needs to be clearly communicated and celebrated.
- The best way to show the world (and the employees) that the merger works, is to quickly announce some new business deals done on the back of the new found strengths, synergies and those differences too. Rapidly-formed task forces and teams from both companies in sales, marketing, R&D, manufacturing etc., can help this process immensely and show that the merger was not only a good idea but a practical moneymaker too.
- Communication becomes super-critical. Quick, accurate, constant and clear, are the watchwords. All too often we see mergers where communication breaks down, isn't done at all or is not done quickly enough. Getting the employees at all levels to understand and appreciate what has happened and to pull together as part of the new business is paramount: communication (lots of it) is the way to make that happen. And it must go on long after that magic 100 day barrier.
- CEO and senior management *must* invest their time. Regular walkabouts by top managers are essential to retain motivation and persuade each side that their own leaders (to whom they will suddenly have become very loyal) are not

3 This research also formed part of a paper 'Human Resources and Mergers and Acquisitions' developed by the London office of human resource consultants, Towers Perrin, 2002.

being sidelined. Top managers should be accompanied by immediate reports to reinforce their authority. These personal forays are difficult to arrange and manage – especially in a cross-border acquisition – because the top team is usually pre-occupied in the early stages: but it is vital to get the human relations process flowing freely, and friendly.

- Avoid the pitfall of mixed messages. Shareholders get told that there will be 'major cost savings' (usually involving cuts in staffing levels), conversely, employees are informed they 'will be treated fairly and there will only be minimal job cuts'. This just creates bad feeling and confusion. The business loses out.
- If there have to be job cuts go deep the first time and do it quickly. There is nothing worse than a constant stream of announcements of redundancies, it creates fear, and leads to plunging productivity.
- Never forget that life can be toughest at the bottom of the hierarchy: senior managers do the deal, then other executives start to meet. Down on the production line this rarely happens. Don't forget that it is the workers in the branches and plants that are the most starved of information, they will probably never, ever meet their new colleagues. So you need to explain why this is good for them and their future and what it will mean for their job security.
- Get that talent inventory completed quickly and make sure you secure the people who are mission-critical to the merger success (at least in the short term). Sudden departures of long-serving executives send a very bad signal down the organization and can quickly turn a merger process sour, not to mention the share price.
- HR professionals need to remind themselves that mergers need not be viewed as a time of uncertainty, but as times of opportunity for staff. Even mildly successful mergers offer growth prospects for staff as the acquiring firm brings a wider variety of available jobs and career paths.
- Management professionals should not forget that 'phantom' mergers are just as hard. Persuading staff in one division to work with another division involves the same techniques as a real merger. Knocking down divisional silos and mini corporate kingdoms requires all the techniques of a full blown merger: and they fail too if they are not managed consistently and constantly.

HUMAN RESOURCES

There's an old story that the only thing wrong with human resources is the people, without them it would function quite well. Sad to say but human resources has

been hit pretty hard in this recession, and is now pared down to a very slim operation in many major firms (see Chapter 4 HR's future role).

Our view is that HR is still having an upward battle in too many businesses to get people issues on the critical agenda. As a senior HR consultant told us, 'what worries me is that in too many dinosaur companies the only people worrying about HR issues are in the HR department'. As we said above, much of the evidence we have collected points to the fact that many firms are operating on a hire and fire basis and are not investing that much in their people. Of course, there are many exceptions, but manager after manager has told us of their disappointment in corporate America and corporate Europe in not doing enough to position themselves as people friendly organizations. We don't know if there is a way to change that, but we suspect it is endemic in many businesses and that people still – in reality – come along way behind managing the numbers – except in certain exceptional cases.

So can HR save the soul of the corporation, or will the rest of the management team ensure it has its hands tied? While there are some definite sad stories out there, we do believe after all that whether it is HR itself (see Chapter 4) that makes the running or some new multi-faceted job position, that people just *have* to be on the strategic agenda. Whether you are brutal and just throw a lot of money at it and get the kind of people you deserve, or whether you really develop the employees' potential will most probably depend on the overall culture of the business. We would hope that more companies than not have learned lessons from what they did in the past. Will it happen that way? Well, our view from what we are being told is that we will have to convince our employees that we are a good employer and that we care about their future. Failure to invest in people cannot be seen as a nice-to-have option. Let's watch and see what happens next.

4

HR's future role

INTRODUCTION

While there seems to be concern about what has happened to HR over the past few years a few things seems to be really clear, which give some indication of where the HR profession is headed.

First, it seems that much of HR's responsibilities have been outsourced (training, recruitment, payroll, etc.), leaving behind a dwindling number of HR people. There is no indication that this will change. As we pointed out elsewhere, this means that the HR professional inside the business is going to have to be a very networked individual, because he or she will have to work increasingly with outside support to deliver what line management requires.

Second, much of HR's future work looks set to be in a nurturing role: helping the best get better and seeking out and developing the right sort of talent for the future.

Third, it will be playing a strategic support role, giving line managers what they need to be better.

Doing all this is going to be tough for the simple reason that there won't be enough HR professionals to do the job and there will be a lot of competition for the attention of the CEO and his team. HR professionals are going to have to be very persuasive and very in-your-face to get the people issues onto the table and get them fully and frankly addressed. In our research, it became obvious that we are looking at possibly three levels of HR involvement – and these will depend very much on the type of corporation. While at the top end HR will have a strong strategic voice and be able to fight in its corner for what it perceives as important, we think others will be sidelined. As we pointed out in Chapter 1, new work models are going to breed new people, with new titles, doing different jobs that cross over existing management disciplines.

> *Coaching is not a 'nice thing to have'. Coaching exists for one thing, performance enhancement. That is the only reason you would ever want to do it.*
>
> VP HR, Automotive industry.

If we continue to think of our businesses as made up of finance, marketing, production, human resources and so on, we are never going to get it right. What we think we may well see – and our interview process bore this out – is senior level HR managers becoming much more powerful across the whole corporation, because they have helped to reinvent how the business is managed.

This we think will be a major issue in the years to come and is probably the only way that today's HR manager will survive into the future – as a reinvented function that has a direct involvement in the day-to-day operations of the business.

We would like to think that the importance of people will be recognized more, and believe that within certain companies that will happen: it just isn't going to be taken up by everyone.

Our view is that whatever label you stick on them, we are going to see a lot more involvement in our people, because if we don't, we are not going to keep them for very long. But, we have just said that we don't think that the CEO and his team take much time over people. They don't. But they can be made to see the value of their people and they can be made to understand that there are (let's still call them HR professionals) talented people who can make a major contribution to making people productive.

So, we don't need to have the CEO involved day to day (good as he or she is) as long as there is someone who can concern themselves with making all these people better. You can call them talent managers, you can call them whatever you like, but somewhere you are going to need them.

Consider this. What do organizations and people want to do, are there any things in common?[1]

People want to	*Organizations want to*
■ Enjoy life and work, achieve success and excel at what they do.	■ Engage the people they serve and enable outstanding performance.
■ Do work they care about; create and deliver financial and human value.	■ Provide enriching products and services; create and deliver financial and human value.
■ Create and express a unique professional identity.	■ Create and build a distinctive corporate brand.
■ Find the right organization and the role that suits them best.	■ Find the best people and match them to the right roles.
■ Use their skills, stretch themselves and develop new abilities.	■ Use the skills of their people, improve effectiveness and drive value growth.
■ Make a valued and recognized contribution.	■ Enable and reward contribution to corporate purpose.

1 Coburn, Tim (2002) *Leadership as Authorship: corporate purpose and personal journeys in the 21st century*, www.personaljourneys.com

All in all, organizations and the people they employee really want the same things. So why do we have to make it so hard for people to do what they naturally want to do anyway: contribute? Maybe we are being just a little cynical (don't blame us our research points to a definite lack of appreciation for HR's contribution), but we think that getting at least some of this stuff right is all about one simple thing – running your business properly. If you happen to find yourself in a firm where the CEO doesn't think he or she is also the senior HR person, don't despair. Well, don't despair as long as someone is taking notice.

The reality – which a lot of firms manage to block by their ill-thought actions – is that people actually want to enjoy their work. They want to do well at what they do. They want to know that they are making a difference and they want to find roles and projects that allow them to use their talent and achieve personal goals. Too bad that we don't always recognize this. Yet in this new world of work, the winners will be those that can harness that enthusiasm for doing a good job.

> *Shaping the organization is critical. Basically our business never looks the same two days in a row.*
>
> VP HR, IT industry.

Our view – and the view of practically all those we interviewed – is that we have to make real efforts to recruit and retain the right people. And we will need to get very good at doing that. In this the HR professionals has a massive role to play (no matter what title is on his or her business card). Think of these as key responsibilities:

- Chief talent officer
- Chief people developer/head coach
- Chief work–life balance officer
- Chief rewards executive
- Chief of culture relations
- Keeper of the corporate conscience.

Here's how some of these will work:

CHIEF TALENT OFFICER

We are facing a talent famine and this role will be crucial. The chief talent officer is going to be charged with the responsibility for finding and holding the best talent you can get for the money. Not only that, with a premium on good people,

one of the keys to this job will be to have enough 'helpers' to locate and sign-up good people before the competition. That means that getting into bed with the very best in executive search and recruitment (because you won't be able to do it internally). That means having permanent searches underway – globally – for top performers. It will also mean knowing the strategic direction the company is going in, to be able to provide the needed human capital at the right time. So, in addition to managing people in, it will entail professional managing people out when they have completed assignments as well as working with a second level of 'contracted' staff, who may well work for other businesses. It is going to be a lot more complex than in the past.

CHIEF PEOPLE DEVELOPER/HEAD COACH

A lot of what human resource-style people will do will centre around getting the people you have already hired better than ever. They, of course, will expect lifelong learning as part of the overall reward process. Additionally, senior human resources people will be expected to make sure that the top team is constantly up-to-speed and know where to access the very best in learning and personal development experiences for them.

HR watch that talent thing

You can take the talent issue too far, and by only concentrating on that, lose out with what you have already. Several management observers have warned against what they have seen as an excessive obsession with the talent issue.[2] What it can lead to they say includes:

- Over-emphasis on rewarding individual performance. Creating risks to teamwork and the creation of internal competition.
- A tendency to glorify external talent to the detriment of insiders. As a result valuable current employees quit and the recruiting task gets harder.
- The creation of a self-fulfilling prophecy. Less-able employees become still less able because they get less support and become demotivated.

Continued...

2 Professor Jeffrey Pfeffer (2002) *Fighting the War for Talent is Hazardous to Your Health*, Stanford University Graduate School of Business.

- A tendency to focus on getting the right people in the door, but not fixing the cultural, systemic and process issues within the company.
- Development of an elitist, arrogant attitude and the assumption that since the firm has the smartest people it 'knows everything'.

CHIEF WORK–LIFE BALANCE OFFICER

Work-life balance won't just blow away, it is here to stay. How you harness it inside the business depends, but those that recognize and celebrate flexibility and diversity will most probably have an edge on the competitors. Having formal programmes that meet, exceed and develop with people expectations, has got to be the way to go. That way, you'll have a more motivated, educated and productive workforce.

CHIEF REWARDS EXECUTIVE

Reward programmes are going to be very different as people seek – and receive – a broader range of rewards based on their present circumstances. Again, the smart companies that allow employees to choose the package that fits their lifestyle will be winners.

More than that, we will begin tying rewards down to whether or not we as managers can motivate our teams. And in case you don't see it that way, smart companies are already doing it.[3]

We asked the question, 'In the future, do you think that at least part of the salaries and bonuses for executives and managers will be based on their ability to maintain a satisfied workforce or create a talented team?'

Yes, it is already happening	26.9 per cent
It will happen soon	32.8 per cent
It is something that will eventually happen	29.4 per cent
I don't think so	6.7 per cent
Not stated	4.2 per cent

3 Result of a poll of 250 HR managers at the October 2002 Richmond Events European Human Resources Conference.

CHIEF OF CULTURE RELATIONS

We've come a long way without mentioning culture. But a good or a bad culture in the company is going to be a crucial measurement device and the people who will use it will be the people who work there. If the culture is negative then you are going to have to spend a great deal of time trying to turn it around. Places with positive culture will become true talent magnets, where reputation alone will ensure a steady supply of the right people.

So often as a change agent, you spend 60 to 70 per cent of your energy trying to get people to do what they already know they really have to do, but don't want to face the pain doing.

General manager, consulting firm.

KEEPER OF THE CORPORATE CONSCIENCE

It seems to us that it is HR, or whatever HR will metamorphose into that will take on the mantle of keeping the conscience of the business. Our feeling is that corporation's need to be able to look back to their history and it seems that HR-related skills are best suited for this.

So, far from being eliminated, our experts see human resources responsibilities as crossing the whole of the organizational spectrum. But it is going to be a very different type of task to fit in all these aspects. The thoughts of our experts are leaning toward the idea that we will see a super-manager emerging: what one senior executive termed as a 'transformer', who helps people work and develop and in the process is part of the ongoing transformation of the business. Because, it is the view of those we talked to that our businesses are not static bodies, but living entities in constant movement and development. To manage these dynamic processes will take people with vision, but also people who value the human contribution above all else.

A QUESTION OF REWARD

Our changing patterns of work are also putting new pressures on rewards, both in terms of salary and other benefits that employees expect. We asked the human resources firm Towers Perrin, to answer some of the pressing questions that

managers are asking and get some ideas of where reward strategies are going in the coming years.[4]

Mike Johnson: Within the area of executive or 'expert' level compensation, do you see this evolving over the next five years and how do you think this will happen. For example, where do you see companies (specifically those in Europe and the US) putting their emphasis, e.g. will it be cash, or cash and a lot of incentives?

Towers Perrin: The corporate scandals of recent weeks and months are giving pause for thought on the meaning of words and phrases such as 'accountability' and 'reward for performance'. Over 100 companies in the US have already committed (September 2002) that they will be charging the 'cost' of share options to their income statements. The International Accounting Standards Board (IASB) is pushing for this in Europe too. HSBC, Boots and Abbey National have said they will lead the way in the UK. We may well see moves towards cash and possibly restricted stock in the next few years.

We expect that the requirement to account for share options is the death knell for broad-based option plans and will encourage companies to take a more differentiated approach to stock grants. Bizarrely we may see more performance linkage of options as a way to minimize the accounting cost of options. It would be cynical to say that share options could suffer any kind of 'set back' linked to the fear that stock markets will not bring forth the wealth creation opportunities offered by the past 15 years and that prudent pay policy will depend more on clean cash.

Companies will continue to wrestle with the conundrum of linking pay to performance at the level of the individual and of the corporation. Perhaps, at senior levels, companies will place yet more emphasis on succession planning and retaining executives through a wider range of mechanisms in addition to pay. And perhaps focus on levels that may be 'in line' with the market 'enough' to the extent that they do not need to be enhanced every year.

Let's face it, the hire and fire way is crazy ... it's like going from anorexia to bulimia and back: it's not only unhealthy, it gives you the kind of reputation you just don't need.

CEO, Transportation industry.

4 The responses to our questions were prepared by Towers Perrin's staff in London in the autumn of 2002.

There is also a difficult combination of complexity. We may be forgetting what we are paying for and companies and remuneration committees will need to re-evaluate. Shareholders will become more involved in decisions on executive pay, not because of cost but on the grounds of principle and perception. I think we might see a sharper focus on performance measures and the auditing of these measures. Of course things might move in an opposite direction – do incentives engender the wrong kinds of behaviour? Some companies may want to re-think their reward model quite fundamentally.

Mike Johnson: Below executive compensation bands, how do you see compensation changing (if at all) over the next five years?

Towers Perrin: Broad-based share options are likely to become a hindrance rather than a help. Pressure to 'fix' equal pay problems is leading some companies to establish tighter rather than looser grading and job evaluation systems. Employers are likely to put more energy into communicating the remuneration package and to making employees aware of the value and what they need to do to maximize value – especially in the light of changes to pension policies. Provided employees stayed *in situ* they would receive a pension at age 60 or 65 based on their final salary. Now the benefit is by no means so clear and certain. We may see share options becoming less common below executive levels because of the impact on the balance sheet. Companies will need to think of new reward tools to help act as 'the glue' in organizations.

Four factors in the retention battle

With HR acting as chief talent officer, it needs to consider ways of keeping employees from the moment they set foot in the organization's door. Here's some that are being widely adopted on both sides of the Atlantic.

- A major German manufacturer has developed the first hour, first day, first week rule for new recruits and proactively asks them about their experiences so far with the firm. They have seen first week departures drop over 60 per cent.
- Several firms have created ways to let employees get a varied look at the business, so they can change roles and learn new skills. They report that often you discover talent inside the business you didn't know you had.

Continued...

- Adopt a 'people never leave' attitude. When employees do go, stay in touch. An increasing number of companies operate an 'alumni' newsletter and claim that by maintaining interest it often gets employees to reapply for jobs. As one said, 'they leave and then they come back bringing new knowledge and experience with them'.
- If employees want to change their work–life balance equation, let them whenever possible. Even if they can only work two days a week, you have invested in them and they are a valuable asset. Technology allows us to manage this flexibility so much better than even a few years ago.
- Show the organization's interest in individuals. If you are able to develop and maintain a culture that shows that each employee is important, that is possibly still the best all-round retention tool. Get all managers and supervisors to realize that.

Mike Johnson: In recent times, we have been exposed to the idea that many of our present pension provisions (private pension schemes) are not going to be adequate for those in work today. How do you see this being resolved by companies and will it become an 'attractor factor' for companies who still provide final salary schemes?

Towers Perrin: Companies need to provide employees with the wherewithal to make informed choices about investment. The new era of Defined Contribution pension plans means that we must all become much more familiar with retirement savings and what it means to be saving for the future. Pension, share plans, bonuses, etc., are all ways of accumulating capital and most employees need advice and help to maximize the opportunities. The point is that employees need to wake up and employers should be aware that contributions into DC plans should be sensible – or if they are not (maybe due to base salaries being high), make sure employees know this and take heed. Companies will not, and generally cannot, underwrite the ever-increasing costs of pension provision. The outcome is that employees will have to retire later, consume less and save more during employment or accept a lower standard of living in retirement. An employer that decides to retain a 'high cost' pension may regard it as an attractor but it's no different from offering higher pay – a possibly more powerful attractor.

Mike Johnson: Another factor in this reduction in pension provision by employers has been the tax factor. Do you see this reverting back as whatever government

that is in place realizes the long-term damage/hardship it can cause and the cost it will ultimately put on the State?

Towers Perrin: Employers compensate for any government's tax policy at their peril. Tax rates go up; they go down. Remuneration policy in general should not be driven by tax – but, take the new tax approved Share Incentive Plan (SIP) – this allows employees in the UK to buy shares in their company with pre-tax income up to a limit of £150 a month. This is a good opportunity to give a tax benefit to employees ... but there is some risk and potentially some cost attached. The trend in tax policy is more likely to be the creation of a level playing field for savings products – with pensions attracting less, rather than more, favourable tax treatment. There is a view that tax incentives are a very blunt instrument in encouraging saving. There is little evidence of any current or future government wanting to recreate the dominant role of the traditional final pay plan and the government could not afford to offer the tax handouts needed to make the cost of such plans attractive to most employers. Provided the State is satisfied that people will stay above the threshold for means tested social welfare, there is no cost to the State of employers cutting back on pension provision. From a macro-economic point of view there is probably a disincentive to encourage more saving now. The important political issue is the growing 'grey vote' and its impact on future policy.

Mike Johnson: The State pension issue isn't a problem for the UK alone – all of Europe has the same issue of a bankrupt social security system. Do you see this being resolved and how do you think companies will get involved in terms of providing cover for their employees?

Towers Perrin: The level of state pension provision across mainland Europe is typically much more extensive that in the UK. You could argue that UK employers have, over the years, effectively subsidized the State (State pension provision is a relatively small pension element for folk who benefit from occupational pensions). Employers in mainland Europe may well have to accept more responsibility (although in Italy and France, for example, the State's involvement in many major employers makes this a bit circular). The cost of State pension provision in the UK can be contained such that is affordable. Where State systems have over provided there will be a painful transition as the current working population pays out for high past State promises while having its own prospective benefits cut. The role of the employer will be around the facilitation of the advice employees need so that they can make appropriate choices.

Hire any CEO with an IQ over 115 and you've got trouble. You don't ever want a CEO who's too bright – that's dangerous. You want a guy who will manage a business consistently.

Strategic planning consultant.

Mike Johnson: Back at executive level, how inventive do you think companies will have to be to attract and retain top talent, e.g. will they need to look at split salaries, consultancy agreements, etc.?

Towers Perrin: If anything employers in Europe and the US are trying to simplify arrangements – the era of corporate governance 'spring cleaning' is likely to encourage this simplicity, so concepts like this move in the wrong direction. Companies may well have to re-think the way they do business and offer more creative packages in terms of giving paid or unpaid time off, sabbaticals, contributions to school/university fees. The question will be: what do I have to do as the employer to ensure that I can hire the best people, make sure I motivate them to drive up shareholder value honestly and keep them?

Mike Johnson: Despite the fact that the 'fat-cat' culture is an easy target, do you see more US-style compensation packages becoming the norm in Europe over the next five years?

Towers Perrin: Companies such as Reckitt Benckiser, BP and BHP Billiton – all UK plcs espousing a US model for pay – will continue to do what they think is right, i.e. delivering high performance which their shareholders support. Will US packages be the norm in five years' time? This depends what happens to US packages. It is not inevitable that European pay levels will rise to US levels – although we have seen many companies (usually the major multinationals) revising their approach to managing pay in a global environment. There are many models of global pay that we see and very few have espoused US levels. In any event the US pay model may be about to change post-Sarbannes Oxley, the Nasdaq and NYSE recommendations.

Mike Johnson: There is already an ever-widening gap between the low pay employees and the highly paid at the top. Do you see this widening in the next five years?

Towers Perrin: It has done so over the past ten to fifteen years; it is not easy to anticipate what will change in the next five years to stop it. Even the 162(m)

legislation in the US under the Clinton regime did nothing to limit executive pay (it limited the amount of fixed pay that does not have to be expensed, to $1 million). Voting of remuneration reports (which becomes a requirement from next year) may have an impact ... but no one can say what is the right level of pay for a CEO. We can only show what levels of pay are awarded to CEOs ... what similar companies are doing for similar roles. Remuneration committees will need to take a very different view to pay if the growth levels are going to change. The question is whether remuneration committees should see this as a social question almost a moral question.

Mike Johnson: Every so often we hear of the job with the global price tag (meaning it costs the same to employ the same person wherever they are located). Is this really a trend that will become common, or are we bound by nation-state taxation dependent on simply where we are living? Taking that a little further, the countries that make up Europe are facing the concept of a standard income tax across the region ... would this have the effect of creating at least Euro-priced jobs?

> *Companies had better understand ways to put a real premium on those who can sell your ideas to a diverse group of people who don't have to say 'yes', because they don't work for you, but their productivity is critical to your success.*
>
> CEO, Interim industry.

Towers Perrin: Mobility of labour will have an impact on the salary market but there are big differences at the extremes – Portugal and Greece v. Germany and Switzerland. Moving folk can be problematic because of different costs/taxes and purchasing power in different countries. Some companies escape the curses of the expatriate (e.g. SAP) by moving everyone around on local terms. This is the basis on which you work for SAP. You are based in Germany and want to work in Portugal, you resign and are re-hired in Portugal. Very few people can command a global rate of pay – a few research scientists, a very few CEOs whom, for whatever reason, are wanted by so many headhunters and companies they can name their price. Harmonization of costs, taxes and increased mobility of people may well lead to greater convergence on pay. Net pay levels and purchasing power parities differ greatly still.

Mike Johnson: Having said that the anomalies in the European system at present provide all sorts of strange 'tax exiles'. For example the UK is a tax haven if you compare income tax here with other countries of Europe. Similarly Belgium has no capital gains tax meaning that thousands of Germans, Dutch and French live in the country for just that reason. Do you see these 'advantages' eventually disappearing?

Towers Perrin: There are tax differences between states in the US. Europe can probably tolerate differences. UK is sometimes accused of unfairness because employment costs are much lower in the UK than say Belgium or France or Italy. Pension is the big problem in Europe and is probably inhibiting mobility.

5

Conclusions

On balance, we think that the most significant part of our research process has been the realization that we are going to have to work within a new organizationally structured world. As we come out of recession we are not going to find ourselves where we were two years ago. We are going to be in a world where work-weary employees are going to expect and demand something different.

If we recall those people issues that kept coming up in interview after interview in Europe and the US it is clear that we are going to have to learn to put our failures behind us and get on with meeting the expectations of what we term our human capital.

We think that the top three critical factors will be:

- Engaging your employees, at all levels, is going to be of paramount importance. If you cannot give them a reason for being at work, they'll (eventually) find somewhere else.
- Managing people who have choices and are seeking true work–life balance. This is here to stay, you had better know how to make it work.
- Making it easier for people to do their jobs. This would seem self-evident, but from what we have heard it isn't. Every business needs to look inside its own walls for solutions as much as on the outside.

Bench strength? Forget it! We won't have the money to do that in the future: better to work smarter with what we've already got.

HR VP, Manufacturing industry.

NEW JOBS

As we said above, we are forecasting the emergence of new organizational structures, but more importantly, we will be finding the right people to run them successfully. But what we have firmly taken on board, courtesy of our transatlantic experts, is that these new organizations will be led by people doing – in part – different jobs from today. As we said earlier in this book, look out for those:

- Corporate integrationists
- Logistic gurus
- Multi-tasking general managers
- Senior level people developers
- Security specialists

- Talent managers
- Communications professionals.

NEW INFLUENCE FOR HUMAN RESOURCES-RELATED SKILLS

We also pointed out that we expected to see very soon some serious roles for human resource-related skills to cover much-needed areas of these newly shaped businesses we will have to work in. These, we suggested, could include:

- Chief talent officer
- Chief people developer/head coach
- Chief work–life balance officer
- Chief rewards executive
- Chief of culture relations.

You know, once you've seen death, plague doesn't look so bad.
VP HR, Financial services industry.

WHAT ABOUT TRUST?

Our other major issue from our interview process was this thought about trust in the workplace and could it ever be rebuilt between employer and employee? Our view – having listened to so many ideas and opinions on this, is that it is going to be an uphill struggle, and as we said earlier, the best we can probably do is:

- Treat people as adults, that's what they are
- Communicate as honestly and openly as you can
- Listen to your employees, it's surprising what you'll hear
- Share your vision of the future
- Make them know they are contributing.

Without getting all of these right, the possibility of rebuilding trust will never materialize. And it is going to take effort to achieve this and be believed that you are doing it for anything other than self-centred reasons. We now know that there

is enough evidence in the marketplace in poll after poll of employees to see that trust is slipping further away than ever.

FLEXIBILITY OF EMPLOYMENT

The other important building block of the corporation of tomorrow was creating flexibility of employment. In our view, this is a vital element of what will constitute a successful, go-ahead firm in the future. Individual corporations will have to decide just how flexible they want to be or can be, but if you don't do it, you can be sure others will. When we are back to near full employment again, employees will vote with their feet for a place that offers more flexible and enlighted employment practices.

REPUTATION AND RESPONSIBILITY

And, of course, maintaining a reputation as a great place to work – and an honest place too, will separate winners from losers. If you want to attract the right people you will need to nurture the right reputation. And that will include the ability to act socially responsibly in your dealing with employees, shareholders, suppliers and customers.

Of course there is a major trend to move to Asia for manufacturing. I would advise every engineering student to learn Chinese.

General manager, Manufacturing industry.

... AND THE BAD NEWS

As we forecast, there will be some problems and some issues that won't go away easily.

- Based on its past record, Wall Street will continue to chase hopeful new trends and watch them evaporate.
- The tenure of CEOs will still give rise to comment and concern and cause problems for employees constantly changing direction as another captain of industry takes the corporate ship in yet another direction.
- Equally, there is little evidence that we are going to get any better at choosing who leads our businesses. Hopefully this might improve, and it might raise the

time that CEOs spend in office and have the chance to build some lasting successes.

- As we pointed out, our experts believe that we have proved ourselves once again a hire and fire society, and this doesn't look like changing too much, despite the calls for increased flexibility and more trust in the workplace. We seem to have had our view confirmed by our interviewees, that good times bring a host of corporate human capital initiatives and bad times see them quickly on the wane. A few companies have proved to be exceptions to the rule.
- We expect merger mania to return, with its attendant cost in human terms. Again, there is little evidence that CEOs and their advisers have learned much about the human elements of mergers and acquisitions, a rather sad reflection on our behaviour.